WRETCHED WORMS

by Kevin Blake

Consultant: Eric S. Loker, PhD
Distinguished Professor and Curator
Division of Parasitology
Museum of Southwestern Biology
The University of New Mexico

BEARPORT
PUBLISHING

New York, New York

Credits

Cover, © Juan Gaertner/Shutterstock; 4T, © Maridav/Shutterstock; 4B, © DiegoMariottini/Shutterstock; 5L, © CDC; 5R, © TisforThan/Shutterstock; 6T, © Stocktrek Images, Inc./Alamy; 6B, © Gado Images/Alamy; 7L, © Swissmediavision/iStock; 8T, © Ian Dagnall Computing/Alamy; 8BL, Adam Cuerden/Public Domain; 8BR, © Historic Collection/Alamy; 9T, © Gilles/AGE Fotostock; 9B, © BSIP/Newscom; 10T, © selvanegra/iStock; 10B, © selvanegra/iStock; 11, © age fotostock/Alamy; 12T, © Paulo de Oliveira/NHPA/Photoshot/Newscom; 12B, © Ian Dagnall Computing/Alamy; 13, © Science Photo Library/Alamy; 14, © Kateryna Kon/Science Photo Library/Newscom; 15L, © Everett Collection/Newscom; 15R, © Sinhyu/iStock; 16, © Vanessa Vick/The New York Times/Redux Pictures; 17, © Science History Images/Alamy; 18, © New England Journal of Medicine; 19, © New England Journal of Medicine; 20L, © Science Photo Library/Alamy; 20R, © 3drenderings/Shutterstock; 21, © NYU Langone Health; 22 (T to B), Adam Cuerden/Public Domain, Dr. Neil Campbell, University of Aberdeen/Public Domain, and Public Domain.

Publisher: Kenn Goin
Senior Editor: Joyce Tavolacci
Creative Director: Spencer Brinker
Photo Researcher: Thomas Persano

Library of Congress Cataloging-in-Publication Data

Names: Blake, Kevin, 1978– author.
Title: Wretched worms / by Kevin Blake.
Description: New York, New York : Bearport Publishing, [2019] | Series:
    Bugged out! the world's most dangerous bugs |
    Includes bibliographical references and index.
Identifiers: LCCN 2018049821 (print) | LCCN 2018050434 (ebook) | ISBN
    9781642802405 (ebook) | ISBN 9781642801712 (library)
Subjects: LCSH: Parasitic disease—Juvenile literature. |
    Helminthiasis—Juvenile literature. | Animals as carriers of
    disease—Juvenile literature.
Classification: LCC RA644.P18 (ebook) | LCC RA644.P18 B53 2019 (print) | DDC
    616.9/62—dc23
LC record available at https://lccn.loc.gov/2018049821

For more information, write to Bearport Publishing Company, Inc., 45 West 21st Street, Suite 3B, New York, New York 10010. Printed in the United States of America.

10 9 8 7 6 5 4 3 2 1

Contents

A Walking Nightmare

In January of 2018, Eddie Zytner and his girlfriend, Katie Stephens, walked together across a sandy beach in the Dominican Republic. Soon, however, they both experienced an itchy feeling on their feet. Each day, the itching became more **intense**. "We were scratching our toes for almost the **duration** of the trip," remembered Eddie.

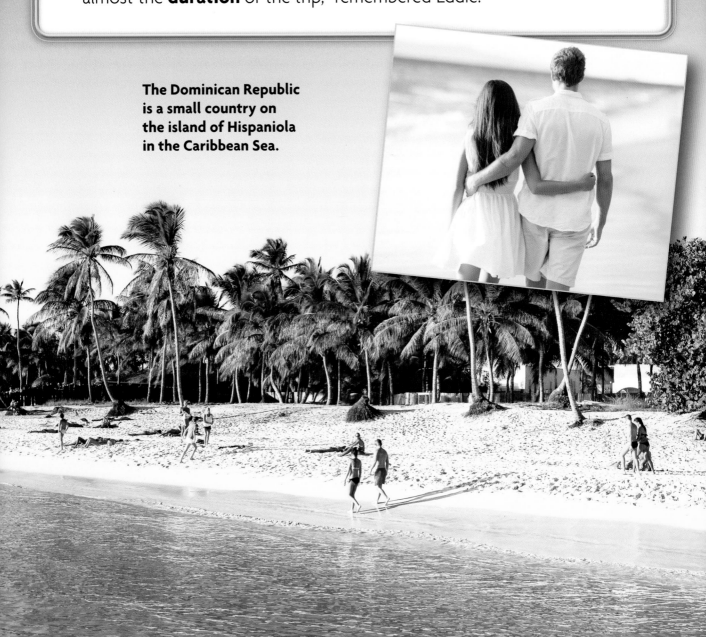

The Dominican Republic is a small country on the island of Hispaniola in the Caribbean Sea.

When the couple arrived home from their vacation, things only got worse. Their feet swelled and red blisters popped up on their skin. The pain became unbearable. Soon, Eddie and Katie couldn't walk without crutches. They went to a doctor, who made a startling discovery. He found dozens of small **parasites** called hookworms crawling through Eddie's and Katie's flesh!

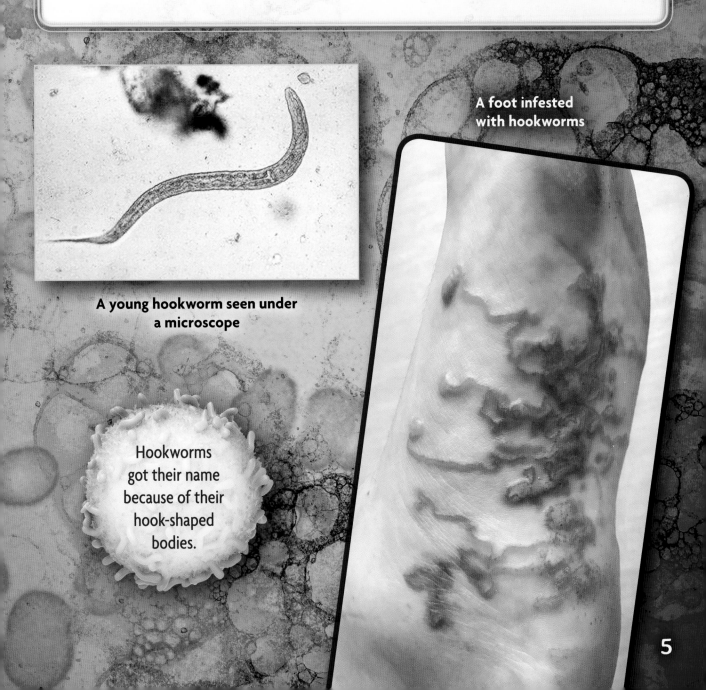

A young hookworm seen under a microscope

A foot infested with hookworms

Hookworms got their name because of their hook-shaped bodies.

Hookworm Life

How did the hookworms get inside Eddie's and Katie's feet? Hookworms are tiny parasites that live inside some people's **intestines**. In the body, they feed on blood and other fluids. Well-fed female hookworms can lay up to 30,000 eggs each day. When an **infected** person defecates, or poops, the eggs pass through the body and are released into the **environment**. The hookworm eggs then hatch into **larvae**. If a person with bare feet walks nearby, the tiny larvae can burrow into their skin, which is what happened to Eddie and Katie.

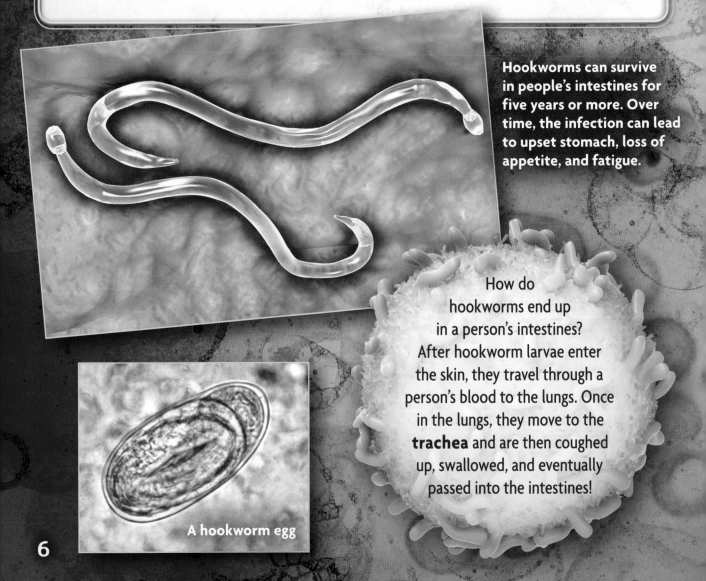

Hookworms can survive in people's intestines for five years or more. Over time, the infection can lead to upset stomach, loss of appetite, and fatigue.

How do hookworms end up in a person's intestines? After hookworm larvae enter the skin, they travel through a person's blood to the lungs. Once in the lungs, they move to the **trachea** and are then coughed up, swallowed, and eventually passed into the intestines!

A hookworm egg

Luckily, Eddie and Katie were given medicine that killed the hookworms. "We've been off crutches for a couple of days now. We can finally put some pressure on our feet," Eddie reported. He advises travelers to be careful. If a beach or any other area looks or smells dirty, "wear shoes!" Eddie advised.

Hookworm larvae thrive in warm, moist soil or sand. It's best to wear shoes in these areas.

Parasitic Worms

The hookworm is just one of the thousands of different types of parasitic worms called helminths (HEL-minths). Others include thorny-headed worms, tapeworms, and flukes. These worms come in many different shapes and sizes. Some are long and skinny, while others are short and wide. One type of tapeworm can grow over 29 feet (8.8 m) long!

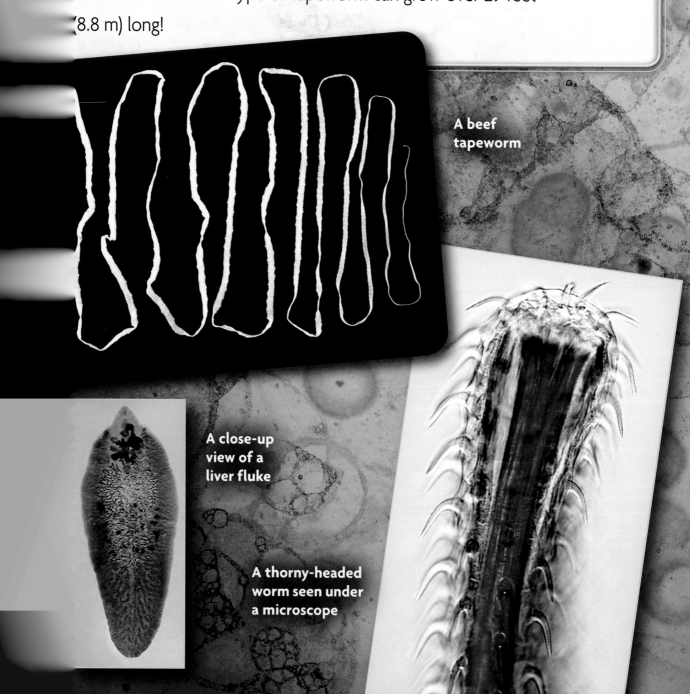

A beef tapeworm

A close-up view of a liver fluke

A thorny-headed worm seen under a microscope

All parasitic worms have three main stages of life. They begin life as eggs and then become larvae. Finally, they become adult worms. However, many parasitic worms have complex life cycles, involving several **host** animals. The liver fluke, for example, must pass through at least two hosts—snails and cattle or other **grazers**—in order to complete its life cycle!

This diagram shows the life cycle of a liver fluke.

Nearly one out of every three people in the world has a parasitic worm living inside his or her body. Around 135,000 people die each year from a parasitic worm infection.

The adult stage of a liver fluke

Surprise!

One type of parasite that thrives in the intestines of humans is the tapeworm. One day in the winter of 2017, Dr. Kenny Banh was working in the emergency room when a patient came in with a roll of toilet paper and a startling story. The man had been suffering from bloody **diarrhea**. After going to the bathroom, he started to feel something strange coming out of his backside.

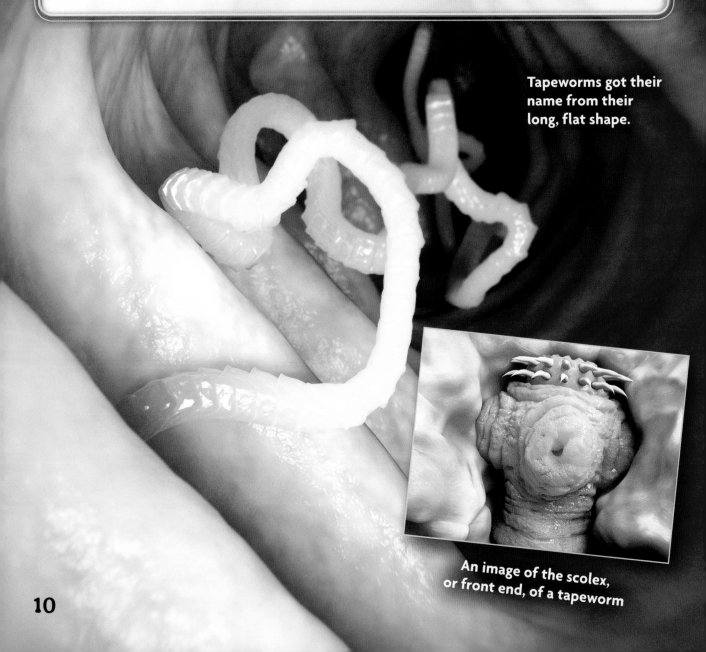

Tapeworms got their name from their long, flat shape.

An image of the scolex, or front end, of a tapeworm

"Oh my goodness, my guts are coming out of me," Dr. Banh heard the man say. However, it wasn't the man's guts at all. Dr. Banh unrolled the toilet paper and discovered a 5.5-foot (1.6 m) long tapeworm! It was as long as Dr. Banh is tall. The doctor concluded that it had been living inside the man's body for years. "It got long enough that some of it was sneaking out of him," Dr. Banh said about the parasite.

A tapeworm like the one Dr. Banh removed from his patient

There are many different kinds of tapeworms. Each kind lives in a different host animal, such as a cow, pig, or fish. The tapeworm that came out of Dr. Banh's patient most likely came from larvae found in the raw salmon the patient ate every day.

Eye Problems

Tapeworms don't only affect people's intestines. They can also infect other areas of the body. In 2018, Sam Cordero, a man who lives in Florida, started having **vision** problems. "I see a little black dot, and . . . something moving from left to right," Sam said. He went to the eye doctor, who discovered that the dot was the larva of a pork tapeworm!

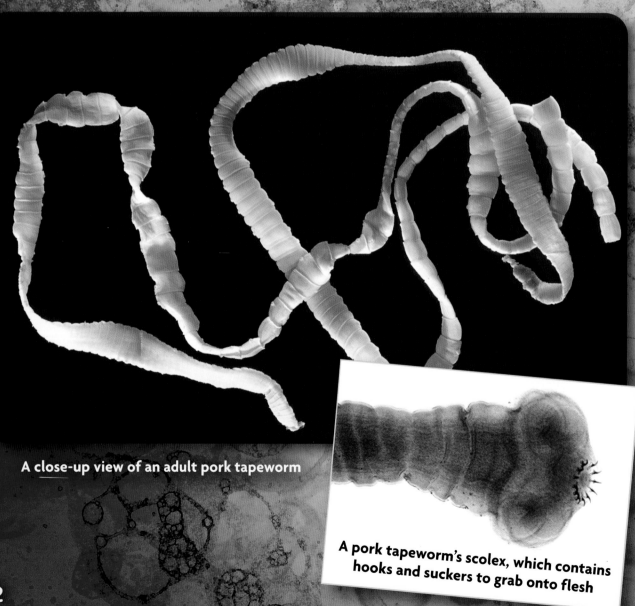

A close-up view of an adult pork tapeworm

A pork tapeworm's scolex, which contains hooks and suckers to grab onto flesh

A pork tapeworm trapped in the eye can be very dangerous, especially if it moves into the brain. The worm can eat holes in the brain, causing it to look like Swiss cheese. This can result in **seizures** or even **paralysis**. Lucky for Sam, his doctor was able to remove the tapeworm before it wriggled into Sam's brain and caused serious damage.

People get pork tapeworms from eating undercooked pork.

Brain damage caused by the larvae of pork tapeworms

A human brain infested by pork tapeworm larvae

Itchy Bottom

Some parasitic worms—like the pinworm—are particular problems for children in the United States. These **contagious** tiny white worms can be spread just by touching an infected person or object and then ingesting one of the pinworm's tiny, sticky eggs. Once inside the body, pinworms take a long trip. First, they squirm into the walls of the intestine and then travel down to the **anus**. There, the female pinworm can lay thousands of eggs.

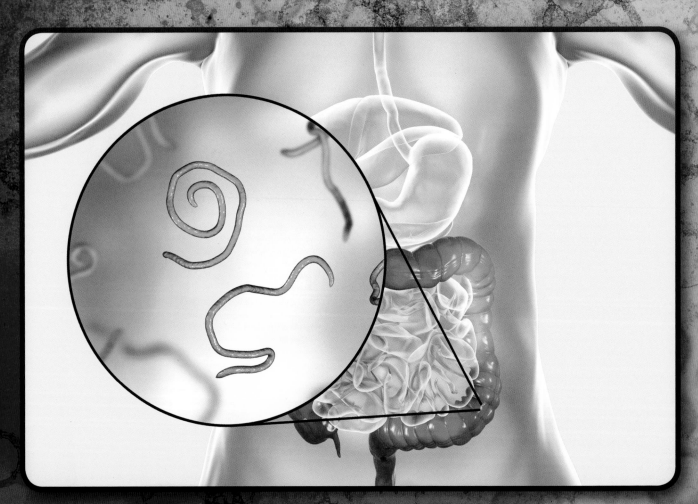

The tiny pinworm only grows about 0.6 inches (15 mm) long. This computer image shows pinworms inside the intestines.

As actress Kristen Bell and her family found out, these pinworms are "very itchy." Kristen first spotted the pinworms after cleaning her daughter's bottom and seeing a little white worm. As with many parasitic worms, medicines got rid of the problem. However, doctors treated everyone in Kristen's family just to be on the safe side. As Kristen learned, the best way to keep pinworms away is to wash your hands!

Actress Kristen Bell

Some experts estimate around 20 percent of children in the United States will get pinworms.

Pinworms in a laboratory

Danger—Filarial Worms!

While pinworms aren't very serious, filarial (fi-LAIR-ee-uhl) worms can cause a horrible disease. It's called elephantiasis (el-uh-fuhn-TIE-uh-suhs). Certain mosquitoes carry the worms in their bodies and spread the disease. When a mosquito drinks a person's blood, the parasites enter the bite wound. Once inside a person's body, the worms **lodge** themselves in the **lymphatic system**. This can cause certain body parts to swell to an enormous size.

More than 120 million people worldwide are infected with these filarial worms. More than 40 million worldwide are **disfigured** by the disease.

Elephantiasis often makes it difficult for people to walk.

Samida, a mom in India, has huge legs and feet caused by elephantiasis. "I had my four children to feed but could barely walk. What could I do? Going to the market for food was a painful experience." Because there is no cure for elephantiasis, Samida was given treatment to reduce the swelling and special shoes. "I am now able to walk up to 3.1 miles (5 km) at a time," Samida says.

The filarial worm that causes elephantiasis, also known as lymphatic filariasis

Under Your Skin

Mosquitoes can transmit other filarial worms, including *Dirofilaria repens*. One morning in 2018, a young woman in Moscow, Russia, felt a worm crawling underneath her skin. It started near her eye. Days later, she could feel the worm wriggling through her lip.

The Russian woman with the worm under her skin

If a patient does not take medicine or have **surgery**, *Dirofilaria repens* worms can crawl around inside a body for up to two years.

The worm has moved under her eyebrow.

How does a worm get under a person's skin? It all starts with a bite from a mosquito that's carrying the worm's larvae, says Natalia Pshenichnaya, a physician who studies **infectious** diseases. When an infected mosquito bit the Russian woman, it left a worm larva behind in the **wound**. As the larva grew, it started traveling around the woman's face. Soon after, a doctor cut open the woman's lip to safely remove the parasite. Fortunately, this "disease doesn't cause any serious problems for human health," explained Dr. Pshenichnaya.

The worm finally wriggled into the woman's lip.

Dirofilaria repens can grow up to 6.5 inches (16.5 cm) long!

Worm Medicine

While parasitic worms cause disease, some people think they may also have health benefits. A small number of scientists believe that certain worms, such as whipworms, might help people with **autoimmune** diseases. These diseases include ulcerative colitis, which affects the large intestine. A University of California researcher named P'ng Loke discovered that some parasitic worms increase **mucus** production in the gut, which can help relieve symptoms of the disease.

Whipworms, like the one shown above, are a type of worm that some scientists think might help fight off disease.

The treatment, however, is still being tested and is not without big risks. After all, parasitic worms can cause serious infections. "I don't think we know enough at this point. We have to do more tests," says Dr. William Gause, an expert on the worms. In the meantime, it's best to keep parasitic worms out of your body!

To avoid getting parasitic worms, wash your hands, don't eat raw or undercooked food, and avoid walking barefoot on dirty beaches.

Dr. P'ng Loke is pictured here with another researcher. Using parasitic worms to treat medical conditions is called helminthic therapy.

Other Parasitic Worms

There are thousands of different types of parasitic worms that can live inside human hosts. Here's some additional information about three types:

Flukes

Flukes are leaf-shaped parasitic flatworms. They live inside the bodies of people and other animals. Most flukes have two suckers—one close to the mouth and the other on the underside of the body. The suckers help the worms hold onto body tissue and feed. People can be infected with flukes by eating undercooked or raw food.

A liver fluke

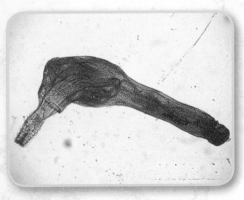

A thorny-headed worm

Thorny-Headed Worms

There are over 1,000 species of thorny-headed worms. These parasites get their name from their long, spiky **proboscis**, which they use to grab hold of their hosts' gut walls. To complete their life cycle, these worms live in at least two different hosts, such as fish and mammals. They rarely infect humans.

Whipworms

Whipworms are parasitic worms that live inside an animal's intestines. They have a whip-like shape and can grow up to 2 inches (5 cm) long. Whipworms can cause an infection called trichuriasis (trik-uh-RYE-uh-suhs), which affected over 460 million people in 2015. Infected people often have stomach pain and bloody diarrhea.

A whipworm

Glossary

anus (AY-nuhs) the opening located at the rear end where waste leaves the body

autoimmune (aw-toh-ih-MYOON) relating to the immune response of any organism against its own body

contagious (kuhn-TAY-juhss) able to be passed from one person to another

diarrhea (dye-uh-REE-uh) frequent loose, watery bowel movements

disfigured (dis-FIG-yurd) the look of one's body changed or ruined by injury or some other cause

duration (dur-AY-shun) a length of time

environment (en-VYE-ruhn-muhnt) the area where an animal or a plant lives

grazers (GREY-zurz) animals that feed on growing grass

host (HOHST) a live plant or animal on or in which other animals called parasites live

infected (in-FEK-tid) filled with harmful germs

infectious (in-FEK-shus) likely to be transmitted to people or other organisms through the environment

intense (in-TENSS) very strong

intestines (in-TESS-tinz) the long, tube-shaped organs in an animal's body that help break down food

larvae (LAR-vee) the young, immature wormlike form of some insects and other animals

lodge (LOJ) to become firmly fixed somewhere

lymphatic system (lim-FAT-ik SIS-tuhm) a system of the body that helps fight disease

mucus (MYOO-kuhs) a slimy substance made by the body

paralysis (puh-RAL-uh-siss) the inability to move or feel a part of one's body

parasites (PA-ruh-sites) living things that get food by living on or in another living thing and often cause harm

proboscis (pruh-BOS-uhss) the sucking mouthpart of many insects

seizures (SEE-zhurz) sudden attacks that can cause a person to shake and lose consciousness

surgery (SUR-jur-ee) an operation that treats injuries or disease by removing parts of the body

trachea (TREY-kee-uh) a tube that carries air to the lungs; it's also called the windpipe

vision (VIZH-uhn) the ability to see

wound (WOOND) an injury to a person's body, such as a cut

Index

Bibliography

Cohen, Howard. "He Saw a Little Black Dot. A Brain-Eating Worm Was Pulled from His Eye." *Miami Herald* (February 13, 2018).

Lieber, Mark. "Couple Finds Worms in Their Feet after a Beach Vacation." CNN.com (February 2, 2018).

Read More

Markovics, Joyce L. *Tiny Invaders! Deadly Microorganisms (Nature's Invaders).* North Mankato, MN: Capstone (2014).

Stewart, Amy. *Wicked Bugs: The Meanest, Deadliest, and Grossest Bugs on Earth.* Chapel Hill, NC: Algonquin (2017).

Learn More Online

To learn more about parasitic worms, visit
www.bearportpublishing.com/BuggedOut

About the Author

Kevin Blake lives in Providence, Rhode Island, with his wife, Melissa, his son, Sam, and his daughter, Ilana.
He has written many nonfiction books for kids.